HOW TO JUGGLE

Have Fantastic Fun While
Mastering the Basics of Juggling

by Steve Thomson
aka Stevie Vegas

How to Juggle:
Have Fantastic Fun While Mastering the Basics of Juggling
by Steve Thomson aka Stevie Vegas

Photo previous page copyright © East Northant Council

Published by:
Mud Puddle, Inc.
36 W. 25th Street
New York, NY 10010
info@mudpuddleinc.com

ISBN: 978-1-60311-667-1

Art Direction and Project Management by Shay Design
Copy Editor - Amber Demien

Printed in China, April 2021

13 15 17 18 16 14 12

3

TABLE OF CONTENTS

CHAPTER 3:

CHAPTER 4:

INTRODUCTION

Photo © Ian Hutchinson

WHY JUGGLE?

There are so many great things about juggling, but here are my top three reasons:

1. You make lots of new and wonderful friends. You can find your nearest juggling club by visiting *www.jugglingedge.com/clublistings.php* and typing in your postcode/zip code.

2. Juggling is great exercise. All that bending down to pick up the object you've dropped so you can try again is exercising with an end goal!

3. You'll never run out of things to practice with! Once you have learned your first three ball tricks, there are thousands more to choose from—then there are scarves, rings, and clubs! Then, you can do all these tricks while balanced on a unicycle or with the props glowing in the dark or even on fire (the props, that is, not you)!

BENEFITS OF LEARNING TO JUGGLE

I could have written a book on this subject alone, but it wouldn't have been as fun as this one, so here are some very brief explanations, all of which can be backed up with research that can be easily found on the internet.

EDUCATIONAL BENEFITS

- **Mathematics Skills:** Math is used in counting throws, setting targets, working out the percentage of successful throws, etc. Research "siteswaps" to learn more about juggling and mathematics.

- **Problem Solving:** Every trick is unique. Books and video tutorials will help you to work out the best way to learn the trick, taking it one step at a time.

- **Appreciation of the Arts:** Now when you see people using their skills on TV or in the theater, you can appreciate the amount of hard work and dedication they have put into their chosen talent!

- **Concentration:** You learn to focus on each part of the trick that needs to be mastered.

- **Imagination & Creativity:** You can let your imagination run wild and experiment with the tricks you have learned. You may end up inventing a new trick just by imagining different patterns that may be possible!

PHYSICAL BENEFITS

Physical Fitness: Juggling is a great way to exercise! Because it is fun, people spend hours practicing. Think of the many times a beginner will bend over to pick up a dropped juggling item; these are bending and stretching exercises. People learning to juggle scarves get a fantastic cardiovascular and pulmonary workout. The repetitive motions of throwing and catching build and tone muscles.

- **Hand-Eye Coordination:** Juggling develops hand-eye coordination, and this will benefit any other sport or skills-based activity you do.

Balance: Your physical balance can improve if you master the rola-bola, tightrope, or unicycle. Your mental balance can improve because these activities use both sides of the brain, so your body and mind will be working in perfect harmony!

• **Stress Relief:** Juggling encourages a mental and physical state known as relaxed concentration in which the mind and body are able to be focused and alert while remaining calm and relaxed. Of course, if you are a professional juggler, then you may find that you need another hobby to relieve stress instead!

SOCIAL BENEFITS

• **Confidence:** Juggling can be learned quickly and is a very rewarding activity that transforms feelings of "That's impossible" into "What's next?"

• **Self Esteem:** When students nail a new trick or perform in front of an appreciative audience, self-esteem soars, which will help them cope with the difficult times that life sometimes brings.

• **Kinesthetic Learning:** If you are the sort of student who prefers to learn by doing rather than by sitting behind a desk with pen and paper, then you will most likely excel at this skill.

- **Persistence & Perseverance:** When you juggle you inevitably drop, but you will move past these drops by persevering with the trick until you conquer it. All of a sudden, drops/mistakes won't matter, as they are just stepping stones on the way to success.

- **Communication & Teamwork:** A beginning juggler who is learning new tricks will show more empathy toward a pupil than any seasoned juggler. Performing in front of an audience improves communication and can help students overcome stage fright, fear of public speaking, and improve confidence—fantastic life skills to possess in any profession.

WHAT YOU WILL FIND IN THIS BOOK

This book will offer a brief history of juggling through the ages, before moving swiftly on to teaching you how to juggle with scarves, balls, rings and clubs. Each trick includes step-by-step instructions and plenty of illustrations to help you. There are also author's notes for extra help, as well as practice points and sections on body posture and mindset. The final chapter will focus on putting together your own juggling show!

11

CHAPTER 1

HISTORY OF JUGGLING

THE ORIGIN OF JUGGLING

The oldest known record of toss juggling (throwing objects in a pattern in the air) was discovered painted on a wall in the Beni-Hassan tomb of an unknown Egyptian prince who lived between 1994–1781 BC. The painting depicted women juggling small round objects (probably balls), one of whom is juggling with her arms crossed over (a trick called reverse arms, which you can learn later in this book).

The word "juggling" is derived from the Middle English "jogelen," which simply means "to entertain by performing tricks". Another variation comes from the French word "jogler," which means "to joke or jest".

JUGGLING ACROSS THE WORLD & THROUGH THE AGES

During the reign of the Romans (753 BC to 476 AD), jugglers were held in high esteem. The Circus Maximus was the first circus established in Rome. It was a huge open air arena with a large oval ring. There was enough space for over 250,000 spectators, so it was enormous! The arena was used for chariot races, horse shows, battle re-enactments and other entertainment. Trained exotic animals were also on display. Acrobats and jugglers entertained the audience between the main events.

When the Roman Empire fell, the circus also disappeared. Over the next 1,000 years, showmen and small groups of entertainers wandered from town to town. Bands of wandering minstrels kept the skills of the circus alive throughout the 14th and 15th centuries.

Around the 16th century, these wandering minstrels and traveling communities came to be considered as no better than worthless beggars who practiced evil and sorcery. No longer able to wander freely, they usually entertained at county fairs and other places designed specifically for performing.

It wasn't until the late 18th century that the circus returned as an exhibition of horses, acrobatics and other performances. Philip Astley is thought to have established the first permanent traveling circus, which was a huge hit in London, where the first performance took place in 1768. He also realized that instead of performing his equestrian (horse) acts in a linear fashion (galloping along beside a line of spectators), he could make more money by training the horses to gallop in a ring within a performance area surrounded by tiered seats. German and Italian tent makers, and later French manufacturers, were responsible for new tent and seating systems that made many European traveling circuses almost as comfortable and efficient as any show in a permanent building.

During this period, horse riding was the biggest attraction of a circus show. In 1793, John Bill Rickets presented America's first circus. In his opening show, watched by President George Washington, Ricketts juggled while on the back of a horse!

Jugglers were in great demand in the 19th century, when variety and music hall theaters were popular in Europe, and vaudeville was at its height in North America. Jugglers provided "front of curtain" entertainment while the sets or acts were changed behind the curtain.

In Russia in 1927, the State University of Circus and Variety Arts was founded by the government at the request of Lenin; it later became known as the Moscow Circus School. The university taught gymnastics, and the gymnasts began touring in the 1950s, which was an amazing success and changed how modern circuses would progress.

In the 1940s, Ringling Brothers Barnum and Bailey Circus in America required 109 railway carriages to transport up to 1,400 people, plus hundreds of animals and their gigantic four-ring big-top tent, which could seat over 10,000 paying customers!

FAMOUS JUGGLERS

Paul Cinquevalli (1859–1918)

Known as The Human Billiard Ball Table, his nickname refers to a favorite trick that involved juggling and rolling balls all over his body, before catching them in special pockets on his green felt jacket. Cinquevalli invented many tricks, especially manipulating any objects that weren't nailed to the floor (chairs, hats, umbrellas, etc.)! One of his most dangerous tricks was catching a wooden washtub (20 kg) on his head!

Enrico Rastelli (1896–1931)

Rastelli was able to juggle ten balls, eight sticks, and eight plates (although not at the same time). His dedication and mastery of these particular props led to their popularity in juggling.

Bobby May (1907–1981)

May was known as The International Juggler. Although he could juggle eight balls, his best routines were with three and five balls. The routines contained bounce moves with added spin so the balls would bounce back unexpectedly. He could also ice skate while juggling!

Francis Brunn (1922–2004)

Brunn left Germany to join the Ringling Brothers Circus in America. One of the first jugglers to realize that although he could juggle great numbers of objects (he is believed to be the first to juggle ten rings), it could be far more entertaining to work with a smaller numbers of props, such as a single ball.

Lottie Brunn (1925–2008)

Generally considered as one of the fastest female jugglers of all time. By the age of 14, she could perform with eight rings.

Anthony Gatto (1973–)

Holder of most Numbers Juggling world records at some point. He joined Cirque Du Soleil from 2010-2012, then retired from juggling and set up a Concrete Business. We hope that one day he will resurface and join us again.

Flying Karamazov Brothers (founded 1973)

A juggling and comedy troupe who perform in theaters all over the world. They are well known for their "Danger/Terror" trick, in which they gradually introduce nine items (ukulele, skillet, fish, egg, block of dry ice, salt shaker, cleaver, torch and bottle of champagne), and then juggle them all at once, ending the trick with a cooked fish, the egg in the skillet and drinking the champagne!

Cirque du Soleil (founded 1984)

Meaning "Circus of the Sun," this Canadian circus is currently the largest theatrical production company in the world, making profits in the hundreds of millions each year. Their shows are a wonderful mixture of circus styles from all around the world, with a solid theme at the core.

Gandini Juggling Project (founded 1992)

Created by Sean Gandini and Kati Ylä-Hokkala, they have been at the forefront of making juggling modern and relevant for the 21st century with their touring shows. Their juggling workshops are also very inspiring and challenging no matter how expert a juggler you might think you are.

Jay Gilligan

An American juggler who now lives and performs mainly in Europe. One of the most creative modern-day jugglers you are likely to find. (Watch some of Jay's "TEDTalks" on YouTube—you won't be disappointed!")

Wes Peden (1990–)

From 2007–2010, Peden studied at Circus University in Stockholm, where his head juggling professor was Jay Gilligan! He holds various world records for five to seven club tricks, and his inspirational juggling videos and shows at juggling conventions all over the world are showing the next generation of jugglers what new possibilities are out there.

The list could go on and on, but please spend some time searching for more information on:

Trixie Larue, Team Rootberry, Cindy Marvell, Alex Barron, Kris Kremo, Stefan Sing, Steve Rawlings, Felix Sürbe, Vova and Olga Galchenko, Sergei Ignatov, Thom Wall and Stevie Vegas (oaky, the last name is me, but when else am I going to be able to put myself among such esteemed company?).

WORLD RECORDS

The following world records are from the official Guinness World Records website.

Most Objects Juggled

These are qualifying records. To "qualify" with a certain number, you need to catch each object at least twice. To "flash" requires just one catch of each object.

- Alex Barron (UK) 2017: Eleven balls. He has also flashed twelve, thirteen and fourteen balls, so maybe one day we will have a new world record!

- Anthony Gatto (US) 2005: Ten rings. Albert Lucas (US) was able to flash thirteen rings back in 2002.

- Anthony Gatto (US) 2006: Eight clubs. Willy Colombaioni (US) has video footage of also qualifying eight clubs in 2015.

Other Juggling World Records

- David Rush (US): 556 catches of three balls in one minute.

- Ian Stewart (CAN): Three chainsaws, ninety-four catches.

- Quinn Spicker (CAN): Twelve minutes, fifty seconds— Longest Duration Juggling of Three Objects While Suspended Upside Down.

USEFUL RESOURCES

To learn more about the history of juggling:

- Visit the Museum of Juggling History or their website at *historicaljugglingprops.com*. The museum is curated by David Cain, who currently holds twenty world records and is also known as "Juggler for Jesus."

- Visit the International Juggling Association website at *www.juggle.org*.

- To find juggling clubs and conventions, visit The Juggling Edge at *www.jugglingedge.com*.

Photo © Mark Bond

CHAPTER 2:

JUGGLING BASICS

GETTING THE MOST OUT OF YOUR PRACTICE SESSIONS

The tricks in this book are arranged by skill level, starting with the easiest props to learn.

SCARVES ⇨ BALLS ⇨ RINGS ⇨ CLUBS

It is best to practice indoors if possible, although you will need high ceilings and good lighting. When practicing outdoors, the sun may get in your eyes or a sudden breeze could interfere with your props.

Wear loose clothing because you are going to be bending down to pick up your props a lot! Juggling is a form of exercise and quite a workout, so have plenty of fluids nearby, as well as a towel to wipe that sweat off your forehead! Warm-up before launching into the tricks. Stretch your hands, wrists, arms, shoulders, neck and back muscles so they are warmed up and ready for catching your next awkward throw.

Juggling is also a mental activity that requires focus, so turn your phone to silent (or even better, keep it out of the room). You need to "get in the zone," and that is impossible if your phone is making a noise every few seconds!

Mindset

This might be the most important section in the entire book. When you learned to walk, you didn't take a step, fall over and resolve never to try again; otherwise, you would still be crawling! When you learned to swim, you didn't give up after the very first stroke, or else you could have drowned! Mindset is incredibly important when learning a new skill.

Dropping is a Sign of Progress!

I am proud to state that since becoming a juggler, I have made at least three million drops! No need to send me a congratulations card (unless you put money inside it … I'm never too proud to beg!). My point is that only through practice and perseverance will you achieve these tricks, and then you have to prepare yourself for the next trick and do it all over again! If you are struggling, then reach out to another juggler who can offer plenty of advice.

Juggling Terminology

Most of the juggling terms are explained as you go through the book, but here is a bit of extra explanation for some of them.

Cascade

A pattern where the objects are thrown in a pattern that looks like an infinity sign or a sideways figure-eight. This is the first juggling trick I will be teaching in each section of this book for scarves, balls, rings and clubs.

Claw

When you catch an object from above, with your palms facing the floor. The main way of catching scarves.

Clubs/Pins

Long juggling objects that have to be flipped end over end to catch once again. These words are interchangeable.

Columns

Throws in a straight line (up and down) that are usually caught in the same hand again.

Combination Trick

When your trick involves at least two different props, such as unicycling while juggling, or spinning a plate while juggling three balls in the other hand.

Dominant/Subordinate Hand

Unless you are equally skilled with each of your hands, then your dominant hand is usually the one you write with. Once you have learned a trick with your dominant hand, you should then learn it with your subordinate hand.

Doubles, Triples, Quadruples

The number of times an object spins end over end before being caught again.

Drop

When the ball hits the floor. Don't worry, there is a section later in the book that will help you and your future audience to cope with this very issue!

Drop Lines

A funny thing you can say to the audience if you drop during the show.

Flash

To catch each prop successfully at least once. Some performers will also flash their objects extra high and try to pirouette (turn 360 degrees) before continuing the trick.

Nailing a Trick

When you are happy with your success rate at a trick (and when you think it is ready to be performed in front of an audience), you are said to have "nailed it".

Pattern/Trick

A series of moves that look awesome. These words are interchangeable.

Pirouette

To turn a complete circle with your body. Usually done after flashing three objects in the air, high enough to do a 360-degree turn before continuing the pattern.

Qualify

To make two successful catches of each object. For example, to qualify seven balls, you need at least fourteen catches.

Sync/Off-sync

Sync refers to synchronized, which means that both hands throw at the same time. Off-Sync is the opposite, where objects are thrown at different times from each hand.

OBJECTS YOU CAN JUGGLE

The Flying Karamazov Brothers have a routine in their show called "The Challenge". Audience members are asked to bring along an object they would like The Champ to juggle. Three objects are picked based on audience cheers, and the only rules are that the object must:

1. Weigh between 28–4,500 grams

2. Be no bigger than a bread box

3. No live animals or dangerous objects (such as a mousetrap)

Their routine was based on the assumption that if you can juggle with scarves, balls, rings and clubs, then any object that fits the above criteria will behave like a combination of these objects. When reading through the tricks in Chapter 3, you will discover that many of the tricks can be done with all of these objects. Here is a quick summary of what makes each of the standard juggling props unique.

- **Scarves:** These will float gently in the air, which is why I teach this prop before any of the others. Having a bit of extra time to consider your next throw helps you to not panic. Scarves are almost always caught in a clawing motion, with your palm facing the floor.

- **Balls:** The prop most likely to roll underneath the couch! It is easier to fit more balls in your hand than rings or clubs, which may explain why the world record for balls is the highest.

- **Rings:** These can be flipped end over end (pancake throws), juggled flat or sideways toward the audience; each approach gives a totally different perspective to each trick. Rings can also be stacked around the neck or thrown along the floor with backspin so they will return to you.

- **Clubs:** When placed on the floor, they will roll in a perfect circle around your body (called club rolling). A club can be balanced on another club. You can spin the club just once, or you can do doubles, triples and quadruples.

Photo © Steve Beeston

CHAPTER 3:

JUGGLING TRICKS &
STEP-BY-STEP INSTRUCTIONS

BODY POSITION

Body position is the first step before starting your juggling practice. Stand up, place your feet about shoulder width apart and bend your knees slightly. For most juggling tricks, your arms should be bent at the elbow and held just a little out from the side of your body.

Try to imagine your juggling practice is taking place inside an elevator, which means you have a limited amount of space for your throws. Your throws can't go too far to your left or right. There's not much space in front of you, so you can't walk forward as you juggle (one of the biggest bad habits that newbies make). You also can't throw too high, which is very important because the higher you are able to throw an object, the farther away from you it can go, which means you will be chasing your objects all over the place.

SCARF JUGGLING

It is best to learn juggling with scarves before moving on to balls, if possible. It is the same first pattern (cascade) for all four of the main juggling props (scarves, balls, rings and clubs), and scarves allow your brain to get used to this pattern without panicking, as each throw can be nice and slow with time to think of the next move.

THREE SCARF CASCADE

STEP 1: One Scarf

1. Hold the scarf at one corner in your dominant hand.

2. Lift your arm as high as you can across your body and toss the scarf with the palm of your hand facing outward (like you are waving goodbye to someone).

3. Reach high up with your other hand and catch the scarf as you bring your hand down (this is called clawing).

4. Now repeat this move and throw back to the first hand.

NOTE:

- *Try to make each throw to the same height (peak).*

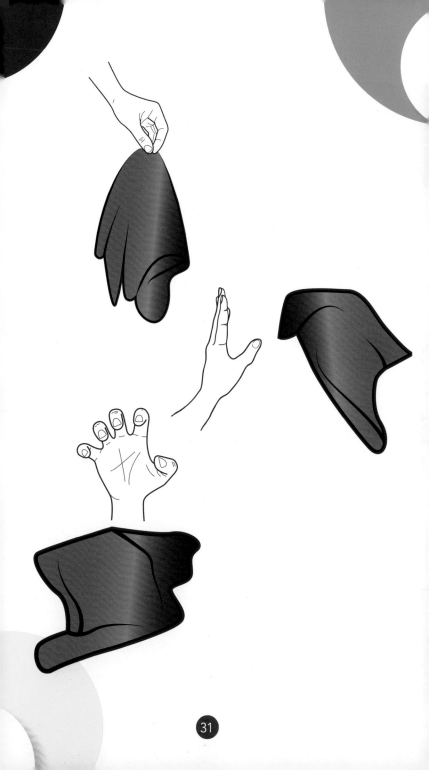

STEP 2: Two Scarf Exchange

Your objective is to be able to throw (scarf #1), throw (scarf #2), catch (scarf #1), catch (scarf #2), pause for a couple of beats and then repeat.

1. Hold a scarf in each hand.

2. Throw a scarf from your dominant hand (the exact throw you learned with one scarf).

3. When scarf #1 reaches its peak (as high as it is going to go), then throw scarf #2 in the opposite direction. The pattern should look like a sideways figure-eight.

4. Catch scarf #1 in your subordinate hand.

5. Catch scarf #2 in your dominant hand.

NOTES:

- *Do not throw or catch both scarves at the same time! You need this gap for scarf #3 to be introduced to the pattern.*

- *Remember to practice starting from your subordinate hand.*

PRACTICE POINT: Carry your props with you wherever you go. This might help you to fit in some extra practice sessions. Scarves are very portable.

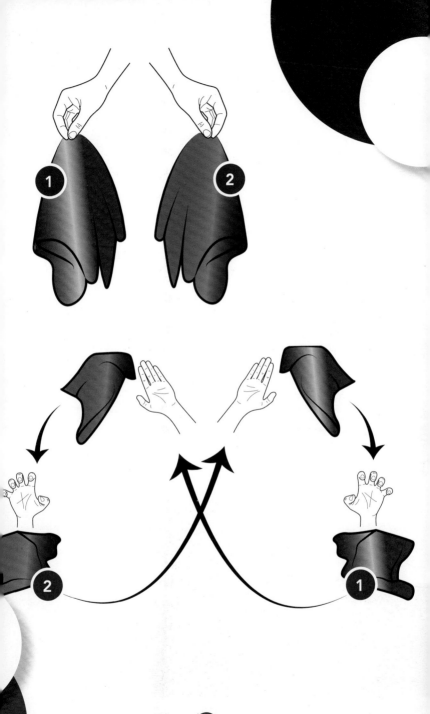

STEP 3: Three Scarf Cascade

1. Put two scarves in your dominant hand (you will need to experiment to find a good way to hold them to be able to make a good clean first throw).

2. Put one scarf in your subordinate hand.

3. Throw scarf #1 from your dominant hand, and when it reaches its peak, throw scarf #2 from your subordinate hand.

4. When scarf #2 reaches its peak, throw scarf #3 from your dominant hand.

5. Keep alternating throws between hands. As your hand comes down after each throw, it grabs the previously thrown scarf.

NOTES:

- *Your pattern must begin by throwing one of the two scarves from your dominant hand, otherwise it will come to a natural halt after just two throws.*

- *If you are still struggling, take a look at the Having Problems section on page 46 in Ball Juggling Tricks.*

- *To qualify as a three-scarf juggler, you need to make six catches. Keep practicing and you will soon be able to call yourself a juggler!*

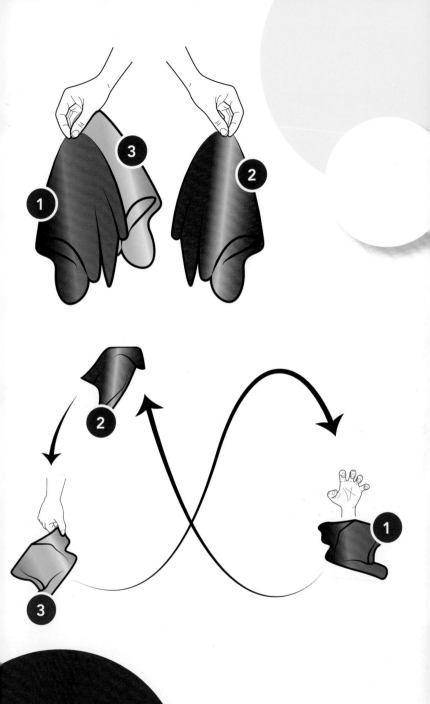

SCARF-JUGGLING TRICKS & BITS

Columns

1. Throw one scarf straight up in line with the center of your body.

2. When this scarf reaches its peak, throw the other two scarves (one from each hand) up on either side of the middle scarf.

3. Catch the middle scarf, toss it again, catch the outer scarves, toss them and keep going!

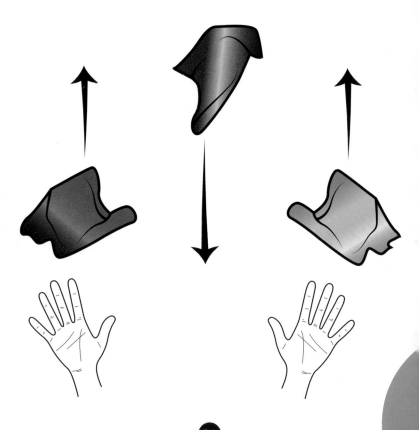

Under the Leg

1. Throw a scarf from your dominant hand under your subordinate leg (for example: throw from your right hand under your left leg). Try to make the throw as high as possible so you have more time to do the throw.

2. Now start a three-scarf cascade with this as your first throw.

3. Throw the scarf under your leg while juggling the cascade pattern.

Under the Leg Variations:

- Every throw from your dominant hand goes under your leg.

- Every throw from either hand goes under your leg (hopping from foot to foot is required for this one, but it looks entertaining!).

- Your left hand throwing under your left leg.

- Your right hand throwing under your right leg.

- Your left hand throwing under your right leg.

Kick-Up

1. Start the routine with one scarf balanced on your foot, and then kick it up into the juggling pattern.

2. Alternatively, during a routine, let the scarf fall onto your foot and pause to accept some applause before kicking it back into the pattern.

Catch Scarf on Head/Headswap

1. Throw a scarf extra high, and then step forward a little and let it land on your head.

2. Land all three scarves on your head in quick succession, and then take them off and continue the pattern.

3. Continually switch the scarf colors on your head.

Forehead Wipe

Demonstrate how tiring scarf juggling can be by throwing a scarf high and mopping your sweaty forehead with another scarf in your hand.

Blow-Up

When the scarf is high in the air, step under it and blow upward to make it rise even higher. It helps if the falling scarf is as flat as possible, rather than scrunched up.

Two Scarves in One Hand

1. Throw two scarves (one at a time) using just one hand in a clockwise direction.

2. Throw in a counterclockwise direction.

3. Throw with your subordinate hand.

NOTE:

- *This is the secret to juggling four scarves (two scarves juggled in each hand, with no crossovers!). See Numbers Juggling on page 82 for more details.*

WHAT'S NEXT?

- Practice more three-scarf tricks.

- Move on to juggling four scarves (see the Two Scarves in One Hand trick for guidance).

- You are now ready to move on to ball juggling!

BALL JUGGLING

Be sure you have learned to juggle scarves before moving on to balls; if so, you should find the three-step process for learning the three-ball cascade very familiar. But fear not if you dove straight into this chapter—all will be explained!

The cascade is the first pattern that beginners should learn with balls. It took me three days to learn to juggle the cascade properly. Some people can learn it faster, and some people take longer, but just keep persevering. If you run into any problems, you may find the answers in the Having Problems section on page 46, so keep at it!

THREE BALL CASCADE

Please put in the time to nail this trick before moving on to other patterns, especially if you're a beginner. This is the pattern you will return to after every other trick you have learned, until you're ready to work on putting together a three-ball routine.

STEP 1: One Ball

See page 29 for details on your body position.

1. Throw one ball from one hand to the other in a large arc that is just above head height. The ball should peak over your opposite shoulder and then fall toward your other hand for a clean catch.

NOTE:

- *Try not to reach up higher than your chest to make the catch (a very bad habit!). The ball should be in a solid plane in front of you, not traveling toward or away from your body.*

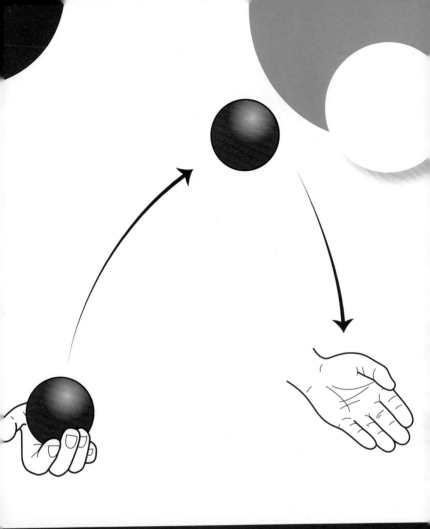

PRACTICE POINT: Where to focus? The best place to focus on most juggling patterns is where the object is about to peak (reach its highest point in the pattern) because the object slows down momentarily before it falls. This position is the bit of information your brain requires in order to decide where to move your hands to catch it.

STEP 2: Two Ball Exchange

Your objective is to be able to throw (ball #1), throw (ball #2), catch (ball #1), catch (ball #2), pause for a couple of beats and then repeat.

1. Hold one ball in each hand.

2. Toss ball #1 from your dominant hand.

3. As ball #1 reaches its peak, toss ball #2 from your subordinate hand in the opposite direction (for example: underneath ball #1). This must also go just above head height.

4. Catch ball #1 in your subordinate hand.

5. Catch ball #2 in your dominant hand.

6. Pause for a couple of beats and do it again. You need ball #3 in the pattern for it to be able to continue smoothly.

NOTES:

- *When this feels comfortable, try starting from your subordinate hand.*

- *Most beginners will panic after the first ball is thrown and pass the ball almost horizontally (or with just a little throw) from their subordinate hand, but this is a habit you must break!*

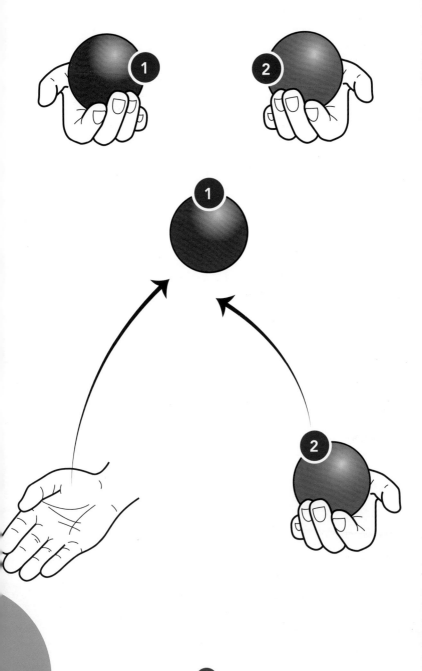

STEP 3: Three Ball Cascade

Your objective is to keep throwing from one hand and then the other in turn. To qualify as a three-ball juggler, you need to make six catches, so keep going and you will achieve it!

1. Pick up two balls in your dominant hand and one ball in your subordinate hand (you will need to experiment to find a good way to hold them to be able to make a good clean first throw).

2. Throw ball #1 from your dominant hand and when it reaches its peak, throw ball #2 from your subordinate hand while at the same time rolling ball #3 (which is at the back of your dominant hand) to the tips of your fingers ready to throw.

3. When ball #2 reaches its peak, throw ball #3 from your dominant hand.

4. Throw ball #1 again, this time from your subordinate hand.

5. Keep alternating throws between hands. As your hand comes down after each throw, it grabs the previously thrown ball.

NOTE:

- *Before picking up all three balls, here is an exercise you can do to help make the trick easier to learn. Hold two balls in your dominant hand. Practice throwing one ball and then rolling the next ball to the tip of your fingers, pause for a beat and then throw it (you don't even have to worry about catching).*

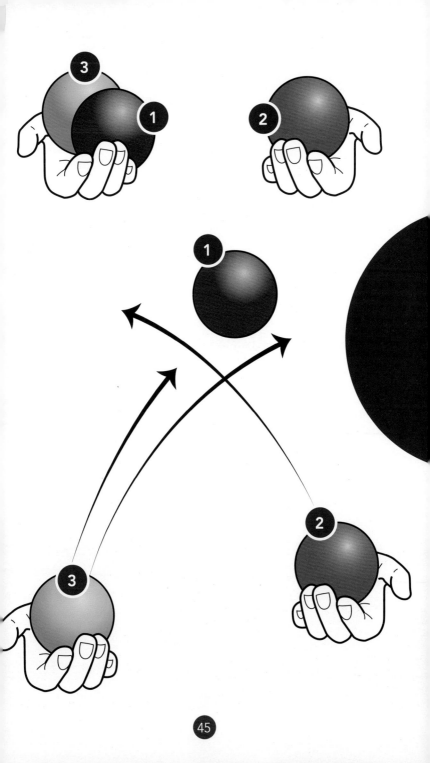

Having Problems With Cascade?

Here is a list of the most common problems you might be running into and, more importantly, how to solve them!

- **Still Struggling:** Practice the pattern with scarves. Practice Steps 1 and 2 for a while, making sure to also start with your subordinate hand.

- **Walking Forward:** Stand so you are facing a wall. You will not be able to run or walk forward anymore, and if a ball bounces off the wall, you might get a lucky extra catch!

- **Can't Let Go of the Third Ball:** Practice throwing all three balls up in the air (dominant, subordinate, dominant), and let them hit the ground. Don't worry about catching them! You just need to be able to get used to rolling the third ball to near the tips of your fingers once the first ball has been thrown so the third ball is now in the ideal position ready to be thrown!

- **Stuck on a Certain Amount of Throws:** Switch the hand that you start with, which may cause you to drop earlier or later than before. You can then keep alternating which hand you start with and increase your repetitions. Count out loud and establish a rhythm. Practicing to music, as long as it is the right tempo, can also be useful!

PRACTICE POINT: Three-ball juggling is perceived as having three balls in the air at the same time; however, most of the time there is just one ball, occasionally two balls, in the air, but very rarely three unless you are attempting to clear your hands so you can do a pirouette. This is good news, as it means you only have to track one or two balls at any given time.

THREE BALL TRICKS

Reverse Cascade

With the cascade, your throws began near the middle of the body, and your catches are toward the outside of your body, but the reverse cascade is the opposite way around: Your throws are going to be made from the outside (so they peak and then fall down the middle of your body) and caught in the middle. Imagine an open bucket centered in front of you at eye level—the balls must be thrown so they would land in the bucket, and you will catch them with your opposite hand.

1. Practice throwing just one ball from hand to hand in the pattern described above.

2. Practice a two-ball exchange.

3. Practice with three balls. Once you have thrown from one hand, your next throw will be from the other.

PRACTICE POINT: It is best not to practice around non-juggler friends, as it might make you self-conscious, especially if they tease you about drops (they may not understand that dropping is a sign of progress). If you do practice in front of friends, you may only attempt the easy tricks you know well (just so you don't drop). It's not much of a practice session when you just do tricks you are already confident with!

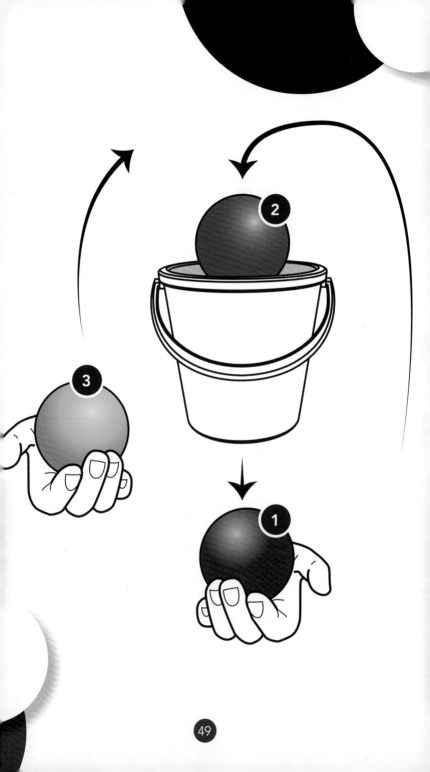

Two Balls in One Hand

There are several patterns you can attempt and they each require a lot of practice, but the good news is that by juggling two balls in each hand, you will eventually be able to conquer four-ball juggling as well as a couple of tricks called yo-yo and oy-oy.

1. For two-ball columns, throw one ball up, move your hand across and throw the next ball up, then return your hand to catch and throw the first ball, and then catch and throw the second ball. Each ball is going up and down in a straight line, just like a series of elevators.

2. Throw the balls in a counterclockwise direction.

3. Throw the balls in a clockwise direction.

NOTE:

- *These throws should all take place in a solid plane in front of you. Your throws are never toward or away from your body.*

Juggler's Tennis (aka Sunrise & Sunset)

This trick combines cascade and reverse cascade into a very pleasing pattern, so please learn those tricks first! The effect looks like one ball being bounced from one side of a tennis court to the other, with the two balls underneath being the net in the middle.

1. Throw ball #1 over the top of the previous ball (in a reverse cascade pattern).

2. Throw ball #2 and ball #3 in the regular cascade pattern.

3. Throw ball #1 back over the top of the previous ball.

4. Juggle ball #2 and ball #3 in the normal cascade pattern.

NOTE:

- *If you have two juggling balls of the same color and one of a different color, then the ball over the top will be easier to spot (for both you and the audience).*

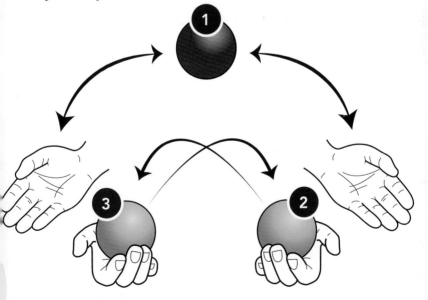

Eating the Apple

1. Juggle a normal cascade using two balls and one apple (or any other food item you wish to eat).

2. Every time the apple is caught in your dominant hand, quickly carry it to your mouth and kiss the apple.

3. Quickly return your hand to its usual position and continue the cascade.

4. When you start to feel confident enough, take a bite instead of just kissing the apple.

5. Try to build up to taking a bite each time the apple is in your dominant hand. It will look very entertaining!

Clawing

The ball is caught palm down on the top of the ball (a bit like when you catch a scarf). You then toss it back-handed, which looks like you are waving to someone.

1. Starting with one ball, do a cascade throw from your dominant hand.

2. Lift your subordinate hand above the ball and swipe down on top of it.

3. Practice the claw using both hands until it feels smooth.

4. Repeat Steps 1–3 of the Basic Three Ball Cascade, but instead of catching you are clawing approximately 10 cm below the other ball at all times.

NOTE:

- *Once you have this trick looking smooth, perform it in a routine and make it look wild and wacky by taking mad swipes at the balls and making your throwing more erratic.*

The Face

1. Just like Eating the Apple, bring a ball to your mouth but this time hold it with your teeth.

2. Bring the other two balls up and hold them over your eyes.

3. Look around the room and hear the laughter!

4. Drop the ball from your mouth, kick it back up and continue juggling.

Body Bouncing

1. Practice a normal cascade, occasionally throwing the ball a little higher.

2. Bounce the ball off part of your body, making sure you rebound the ball high enough to continue the cascade.

3. Repeat for different body parts, and put it all together.

4. Practice double hits (knee to knee, arm to arm, shoulder to shoulder, etc.).

NOTE:

- *Work your way up to this body-bouncing routine: Bounce off left foot, then left knee, then back of left hand, then left wrist, then left elbow, then left shoulder and then head the ball back into the pattern and work your way down your right side (shoulder, elbow, wrist, back of hand, knee, foot).*

Columns

We already practiced a two-ball column in your dominant hand, so now it is time to introduce your subordinate hand.

1. Practice the two-ball column trick.

2. With the extra ball in your other hand, throw it up at the same time and to the same height as one of the other balls (preferably the outer ball).

NOTE:

- Instead of throwing the ball from your subordinate hand, practice a "Columns Cheat": Keep it in your hand and move your hand up and down. Kids love this trick!

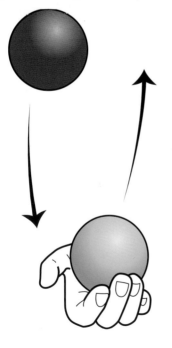
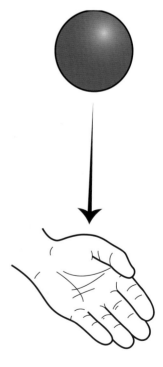

Yo-Yo & Oy-Oy (Australian Yo-Yo)

This trick is easiest to learn if you have already mastered Columns and Columns Cheat.

1. Throw two balls in an elevator pattern (straight up and down) from your dominant hand.

2. Move your other hand up and down, and then all over the place.

3. Keeping an eye on the middle ball in the columns pattern, hold the ball in your subordinate hand approximately 10 cm above it so it looks like they are joined on a string.

4. The Oy-Oy (Australian Yo-Yo) is the opposite of the Yo-Yo, as you need to keep the extra ball approximately 10 cm below the other ball.

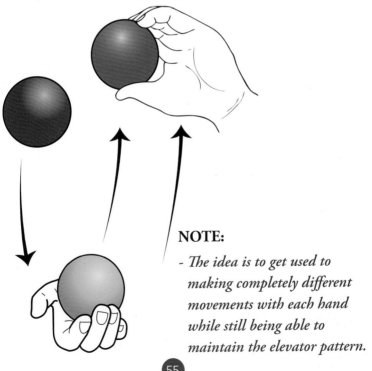

NOTE:

- *The idea is to get used to making completely different movements with each hand while still being able to maintain the elevator pattern.*

STARTS, PAUSES & STOPS

Now that you have mastered the cascade and some simple tricks, the next thing to work on is putting together a little routine. This section will show you some tricks for starting, pausing and finishing your routine.

Starts

Starting a routine can be done with just the three-ball cascade or one of the tricks mentioned below, which are a bit flashier!

- **Two Ball Split:** Start with two balls beside each other in one hand (as opposed to one behind the other). When you throw the balls up, they should split: One ball should go up and straight down again, and the other ball should go across toward the other hand.

- **Three Ball Flash:** Throw all three balls up in the air quickly one at a time, starting with your dominant hand, then your subordinate hand, and then your dominant hand again, grab the two balls nearest to the ground and begin juggling. The third ball acts like the first throw of the cascade.

- **Three Ball Pickup:** Place three balls in a straight line on a table in front of you. Throw the ball on the outside nearest your dominant hand. In quick succession, throw the ball on the outside nearest your subordinate hand, and then the remaining ball can be thrown using your dominant hand. Speed is essential. This is a bit like flashing all three balls in the air. You need to be ready to keep the pattern going once they all come back down.

Pauses

Pausing a routine gives the audience a chance to applaud your efforts. Try the tricks mentioned below.

- **Under Chin:** Juggle a three-ball cascade, and then throw one ball slightly higher than the rest to allow time to quickly put a ball under your chin and catch the thrown ball. Look at the audience and wait for applause! For extra applause, you should be able to throw a ball back up again and then grab the ball under the chin and continue the cascade.

- **Neck Catch:** Throw a ball straight up in the air (not too high and not toward or away from you), duck your head forward, stretch out your arms and lift them up slightly (this helps form a gap on the back of your neck for the ball to land in). This takes a lot of practice. To get out of a neck catch, you have to lower your head and then flick your head back up to force the ball back up into the air.

- **Rainbow Flick:** If you drop during the show, you can pretend it is a pause and do this trick to recover! Hold the ball between your heels. Jump up and kick both your legs behind you, releasing the ball just before you peak. The ball should go up over your shoulder, ready for you to continue juggling. If it doesn't, then try releasing the ball a bit sooner or later, or make your kick-up a bit quicker.

Stops

- Finishing a routine cleanly will show the audience that your routine is over and they should applaud loudly and offer you their hard-earned cash!

- **Flash:** Just like starting a routine, a flash can be used to finish one. Throw all three balls up in the air and then catch them all! If you are quick, you can do a quick spin or grab a hat for the balls to fall into.

WHAT'S NEXT?

Once you have mastered three-ball juggling and the previous tricks, you have several choices to make:

- Learn Under the Legs (see Scarf Tricks).

- Move on to learning to juggle with rings and/or clubs.

- Find some more three-ball tricks.

- Learn some numbers juggling (for example: four-ball and five-ball) (see Numbers Juggling on page 82).

BONUS SECTION: GARBAGE BAG JUGGLING!

Garbage bags are a perfect hybrid of scarf juggling (they are quite slow in the air) and ball juggling (they are shaped like a ball), plus when full of air they take up a lot of space, so this could be the big finish to your show!

To get air in each garbage bag, you have a choice: going solo or involving the audience. To go solo, hold a bag open as wide as possible and spin in a circle. Once it is full of air, tie it off quickly and repeat for the other two bags. To involve the audience, pick three members of the audience to spin around and fill the bags with air—this has lots of comedic potential!

NOTE:

- You only have around sixty to ninety seconds for your entire routine once the third bag has been tied, as the air will begin escaping.

Garbage Bag Juggling Tricks

- Make a cascade pattern as wide as possible so you have to race around the stage to make the next catch.

- Make columns: one garbage bag up in the middle of the pattern and then one on each side.

- Catch one on the back of your head. Bow forward with your arms raised, and catch a bag on the back of your neck.

- Catch the tied handle in your mouth, catch the other two garbage bags and spin around with your arms stretched out.

Jokes for a Garbage Bag Routine

- Ladies and Gents, I am not the worst juggler in the world ... I have not just been given the sack three times.

- This act is not rubbish.

- Well, this act seems to be picking up!

- Ladies and Gents, other entertainers would refuse to do this kind of routine, but I think that would be such a waste.

- I promise not to get too carried away.

- This bag of rubbish came up to me and said, "I'm at your disposal."

PRACTICE POINT: Unless you intend to go into competitions, you are not competing against another juggler, so you can go at your own pace and choose what tricks you wish to learn.

RING JUGGLING

I strongly recommend that you learn to juggle with balls before moving on to rings because it's the same three-step process.

THREE RING CASCADE

STEP 1: One Ring

1. Throw one ring back and forth a little above head height, and catch it in your opposite hand. Give the ring a little backspin to help keep it stable in the air.

NOTES:

- *Catch the ring just before it comes in contact with the skin between your thumb and forefinger, as this will start to hurt after a while!*

- *It's best to practice indoors, as even the slightest breeze can ruin a good throw.*

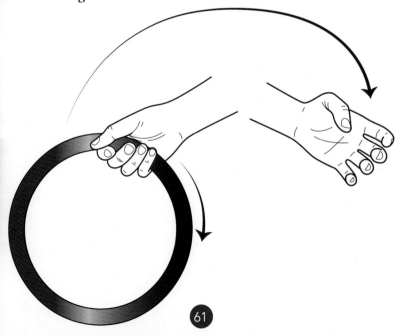

STEP 2: Two Ring Exchange

Your objective is to be able to throw (ring #1), throw (ring #2), catch (ring #1), catch (ring #2), pause for a couple of beats and then repeat.

1. Hold one ring in each hand.

2. Throw ring #1 in the pattern you have been practicing in Step 1.

3. When ring #1 peaks, throw ring #2.

4. Catch ring #1.

5. Catch ring #2.

6. Pause for a couple of beats and repeat.

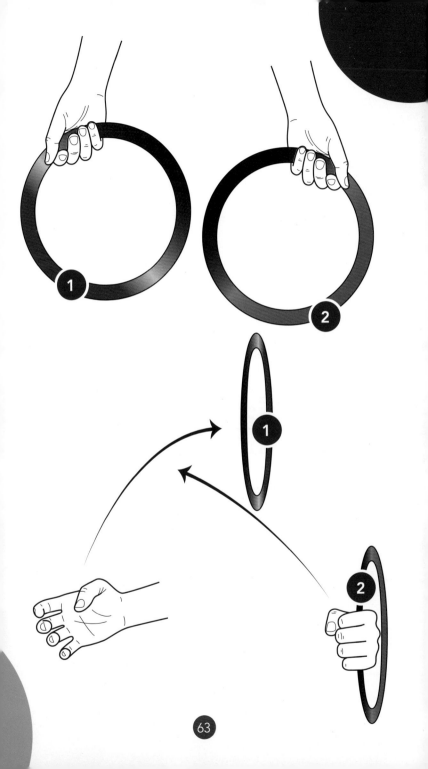

STEP 3: Three Ring Cascade

This trick requires holding two rings in one hand. To do this, one ring should be held firmly and the other ring should be resting at the fingertips. Throw the ring you're holding at your fingertips first, and then use all your fingers to grip and throw the other ring properly.

1. Hold two rings in your dominant hand and one ring in your subordinate hand.

2. Throw ring #1 from your dominant hand and when it reaches its peak, throw ring #2 from your subordinate hand.

3. Once ring #2 has peaked, throw ring #3 from your dominant hand.

4. Every time a ring peaks, throw from the other hand.

5. When you do your next regular catch in this hand, you will now have two rings in one hand that are overlapping each other. Release both at the same time (one ring should go higher than the other).

6. Continue juggling!

NOTE:

- To qualify as a three-ring juggler, you need to make six catches. Keep going, you can achieve it!

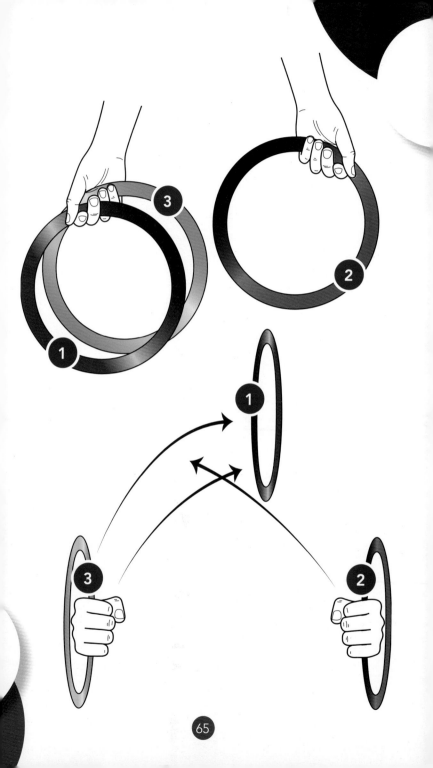

DIFFERENT RING THROWS

It is best when learning these different throws to go back to learning each stage of the cascade once again.

- **Pancake Throws:** Flip the rings end over end, like you would toss a pancake.

- **Rings Facing Audience:** When you face the audience, they only see the edge of each juggling ring. If you turn sideways to the audience, then they see the whole ring. Alternatively, you can stand facing the audience, but juggle the rings flat to the audience (this is the most tricky of the throws to master!).

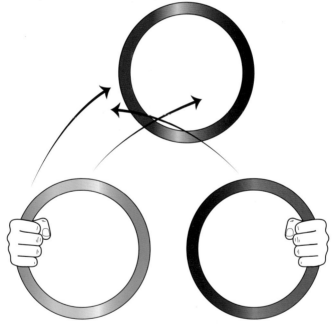

- **Butterfly Throw & Catch:** When you catch the first ring, turn it around so it is touching your arm and hooked over your thumb. Now throw both rings at same time from this hand and continue to juggle.

RING JUGGLING TRICKS

Now that you can juggle a three-ring cascade, go back to the Ball Juggling section and try the following tricks—just use a little common sense when considering the differences between balls and rings!

- Reverse Cascade
- Reverse Arms
- Under the Legs
- Columns

TRICKS UNIQUE TO RING JUGGLING

Stacking Rings Around Your Neck

A good way to finish your ring routine is to place each ring around your neck as you catch them. Safety note: To protect your nose, face, glasses, etc., make sure the rings touch the back of your neck as you put them on and take them off again.

PRACTICE POINT: Try not to track each ball by moving your head constantly. Train your peripheral vision to deal with the whole pattern.

Color Change

The audience will watch you juggle with three red rings, and within the blink of an eye the color will drain completely and the rings will be white! You can either purchase a set of juggling rings that have a different color on each side, or you can tape two differently colored rings back to back.

1. While juggling, catch the top of the ring, with your hand going through the ring.

2. Twist the ring so the opposite side shows, and throw it again.

3. Review and practice the Cascade Steps 1–3, but now with each throw you will be changing the color of every ring.

Ring Grind

One ring is held horizontally and another ring is thrown with lots of backspin and caught on top of it. The spinning ring should be able to spin/grind vertically for a few seconds before losing power. During this time, you could:

1. Throw the ring back up in the air and continue juggling.

2. Toss it up in the air (just a little) and then let it land and grind some more (your trick will last a bit longer if the two rings aren't constantly grinding against each other).

3. Toss the ring up, and turn the horizontal ring over to catch the spinning ring on the other side. How many turns can you achieve?

Returning Ring

You throw the ring in a straight line along the floor and it eventually stops and returns to your hand.

1. Practicing with one ring, snap your wrist toward you as you release the ring forward (this provides the backspin you require). Do not throw the ring too far away from you because it will need a lot of backspin to propel itself back to you.

2. To make the ring come back faster, throw it against a wall or object that is nearby.

NOTE:

- *During a routine, throw a returning ring, and then take a look at your watch or have a sip of water before the ring returns.*

WHAT'S NEXT?

- Experiment with balls and rings together. If you consistently throw a ball through a ring, it's called the Saturn Trick!

- Experiment with scarves and rings together. Tie a scarf onto each ring so you can catch the ring by the scarf.

- Have a cup of tea—you must be exhausted by now!

Photo © Steve Godfrey Photography

CLUB JUGGLING

Before attempting club juggling, you should learn to juggle the basic cascade and know how to do some tricks with balls. It's not essential to have already learned juggling with rings, but if you have a set, then why not?

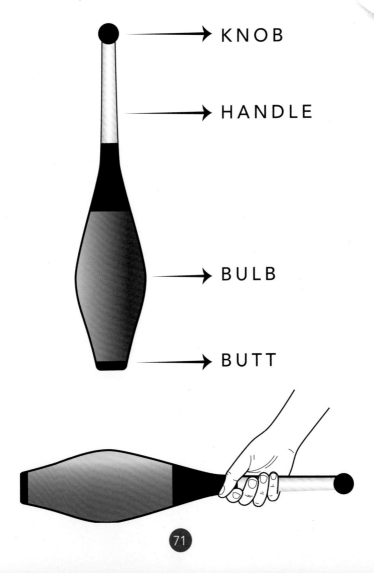

KNOB

HANDLE

BULB

BUTT

THREE CLUB CASCADE

STEP 1: One Club

The club should swing upward across the body so it can be caught in the other hand after having completed a full spin.

1. Practice throwing one club from side to side in an arc that is a little above head height until it is fairly consistent. Throws should not be out from your body but rather upward.

2. Continue practicing throws until you catch the club cleanly every time, which means you have mastered exactly how much spin to put on each throw.

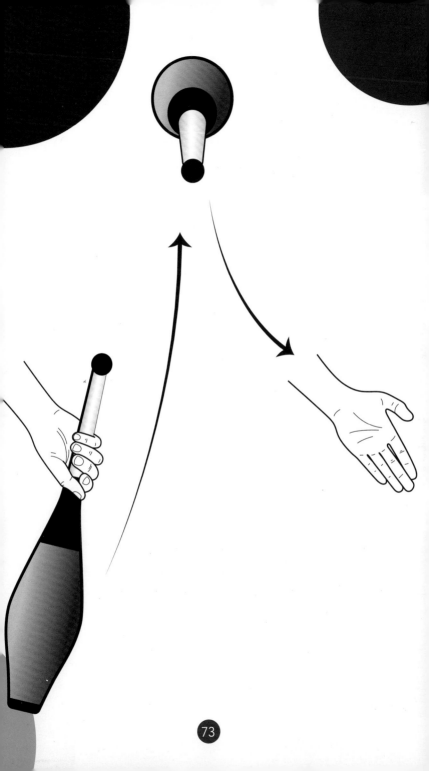

STEP 2: Two Club Exchange

Your objective is to be able to throw (club #1), throw (club #2), catch (club #1), catch (club #2), pause for a couple of beats and then repeat.

1. Hold one club in each hand.

2. Toss club #1 from your dominant hand.

3. As club #1 reaches its peak, toss club #2 from your subordinate hand in the opposite direction (for example: underneath the first one). This must also go just above head height.

4. Catch club #1 in your subordinate hand.

5. Catch club #2 in your dominant hand.

6. Pause for a couple of beats and do it again. You need the third club in the pattern for it to be able to continue smoothly (see Step 3).

NOTE:

- Try starting from your subordinate hand.

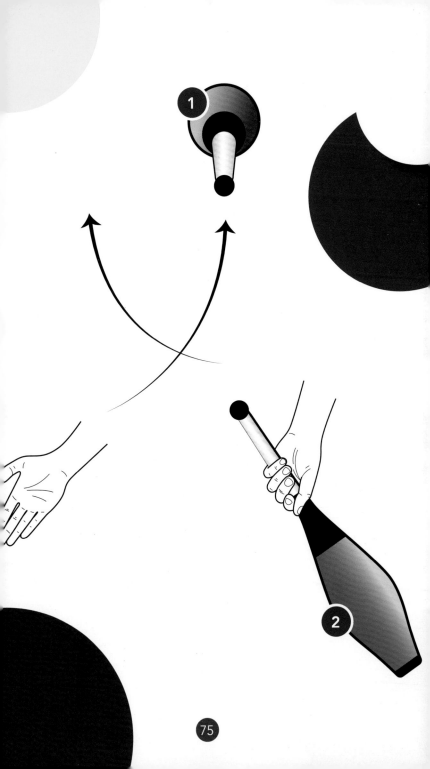

STEP 3: Three Club Cascade

1. Two clubs should be held in your dominant hand and one club in your subordinate hand.

2. Throw club #1 from your dominant hand.

3. When club #1 reaches its peak, throw club #2 from your subordinate hand.

4. When club #2 reaches its peak, throw club #3 from your dominant hand.

5. Keep alternating throws between hands.

NOTES:

- *If you are having any problems, practice Steps 1 and 2, and get your spins as consistent as possible so you are making good clean catches each time.*

- *To qualify as a three-club juggler, you need to make six catches. Keep going, you can achieve it!*

- *For some people it helps to build up to three clubs by using one club and two balls; however, others find this is distracting, as you have to get used to doing two different kinds of throw (a normal ball toss and a club flip) during one routine. If you are having trouble learning to juggle three clubs, give it a try and see if it helps.*

- *You have a trade-off between height and speed. You can throw a high club, giving it just a single spin, and it will look very slow and graceful, or you can throw it low and fast. This gives you a bit of variety with all your tricks!*

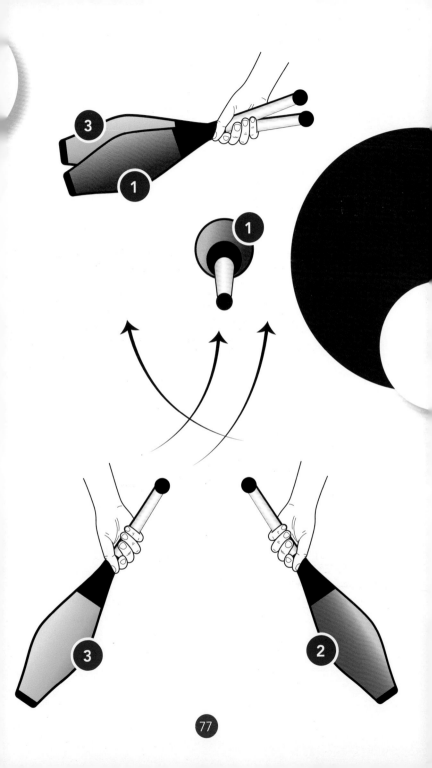

Club-Juggling Tricks

Now that you can juggle a three-club cascade, go back to the Ball Juggling section and try the following tricks—just use a little common sense when considering the differences between balls and clubs!

- Reverse Cascade
- Reverse Arms
- Juggler's Tennis
- Under the Legs
- Columns
- Two Balls in One Hand

TRICKS UNIQUE TO CLUB JUGGLING

Wrong Way Around/Half Flips

In this trick you catch the club by the bulb end.

1. Practice throwing one club from hand to hand with just a half spin.

2. Try this move during your normal cascade routine, and keep the pattern going.

3. Flip the club back the right way around.

4. Once you can flip your chosen club the wrong way around and back, you can attempt to flip two clubs in a row.

5. Flip all three clubs the wrong way around, and then correct them all.

NOTE:

- This trick is one of the most important to learn with clubs because any time you accidentally give a prop the wrong spin, this trick gives you the ability to keep going and flip it the correct way around instead of having to stop the routine.

Chin Rolls

When juggling a three-club cascade, place one of the clubs (upright with the bulb at the top) on your chin.

NOTE:

-The objective of this is not to balance the club, but instead that it should fall into your other hand and the cascade can be continued. It all happens in under a second and looks impressive!

Double/Triple Spins

By giving the clubs a mixture of extra spin, extra height or both, the clubs can have more time in the air, which allows you some time to do other tricks, such as a flourish (explained in the next trick).

1. To achieve a double spin, work your way through the three-club cascade tutorial once again, but this time use double spins instead of single spins.

2. Repeat for a triple spin.

NOTE:

- If you intend to move on to juggling with more than three clubs, then this trick is essential, as most of your future throws will either be doubles or triples in order to give you enough time to get all your clubs up in the air.

Flourish

When you are able to throw a club with double or triple spin from one hand, practice some basic flourishing moves with the same hand, such as twirling the club like a baton, spinning the club on your hand, etc.

1. Practice the flourish separately, and then add it to your pattern.

2. If you juggle two clubs in one hand, then you have plenty of time for the other club to flourish.

NOTE:

- *Work out how best to catch the club so you can go into the flourish immediately; for instance, like you are holding a pencil.*

WHAT'S NEXT?

- Consider putting on a show. If you have worked your way through this entire book, you have skills with scarves, balls, rings and clubs, and a fantastic finale using garbage bags! Chapter 4 will give you lots of useful advice!

- Combine a ball and club. Can you chase the ball around taking mad swipes at it?

- Combine a ring and clubs, and you can finish by catching the tossed rings over the club.

- Replace a club with a toy chicken. It's lots of fun, especially if it squeaks!

- Learn to juggle four clubs (see the Numbers Juggling section on page 82).

BALANCING OBJECTS

Many people don't know the secret to balancing. It is an easy trick and requires just one simple instruction: **Watch the top of the object that you are trying to balance**. Watching the object at the base tells you nothing about where it is likely to fall, whereas the top of the object moves around in a much wider arc and gives you more visual clues that your brain can interpret and coordinate with your body to keep the object upright.

Can You Keep a Secret?

It is actually harder to balance small objects (such as pencils) than large objects (such as broom handles). Tall objects have a higher center of mass, which means they will begin falling slowly, giving you more time to quickly correct your body to keep the object upright. This is good news because the audience will think you are doing something really difficult when you balance a large object, but you are actually making it easier for yourself (don't tell them!).

What Props can be Balanced?

When teaching young children (aged 3–6 years), use peacock feathers, as they are very slow moving in any direction! A balloon on a stick may also be appropriate if you cannot find anywhere that sells peacock feathers. When teaching older pupils, use juggling clubs, as they have a good weight distribution. Broom handles are also really good.

NUMBERS JUGGLING: JUGGLING MORE THAN THREE OBJECTS AT ONCE

Once you have performed some tricks with three objects (scarves, balls, rings or clubs) and you want to learn how to juggle with four objects, you have started on the path of numbers juggling.

The first pattern a person juggling odd numbers (3, 5, 7) of objects learns is the basic crossing pattern called the cascade. A five-ball cascade will be roughly twice as high and feel twice as fast as a three-ball cascade.

The first pattern a person juggling even numbers (4, 6, 8) of objects learns is called the fountain. A four-ball juggler will be juggling two balls in each hand simultaneously without any of the balls crossing over to the other hand. An eight-ball juggler will have four balls in each hand! Practicing with even numbers of objects involves learning the pattern in one hand until it is solid, and then learning with the other hand until it is solid before putting it all together.

When you make a drop, it is usually because one hand has made a bad throw, so you may need to concentrate on just that hand for a while to improve accuracy.

NOTE:

- *You are allowed to skip a number! Some people prefer learning with just odd or just even numbers, so it is quite common for a numbers juggler to go from learning the five-ball cascade straight to learning a seven-ball cascade skipping the six-ball fountain altogether!*

CHAPTER 4:
PUTTING TOGETHER
A JUGGLING SHOW

Not everyone who learns to juggle will wish to perform. When putting together a show, it is vital to learn how to make one trick flow into the next trick.

WHERE TO PERFORM

- **Talent Show:** You will have a ready-made audience who have came out especially to watch some talented performers, and you will only be expected to perform for perhaps three to five minutes. A talent show is a great way to get stage time and improve your skills!

- **Busking:** There is no better feedback than when you busk on the street. If the audience doesn't like what they see, they simply move on without dropping any loose change or notes in your hat. Research whether there are busking laws your area, such as permit requirements or designated areas.

- **Party:** If a friend is having a party, swing the conversation around to party tricks, and then perform your new skill! Offer to teach other people once you have finished—no one likes a showoff!

NOTE:

- *Find out what the floor surface is where you will be performing (cement, wood, carpet, etc.). Flooring will impact how you are able to move around the stage. It's also worth finding out how high the ceiling is.*

PROPS &
COSTUMES

Jeans and a T-shirt don't look very impressive or show that you've made an effort. When I started out, I wore colored trousers (golf stores are one of the best places to find brightly colored trousers) and a solid-color T-shirt, plus a waistcoat. Nowadays, I am known as "The Entertainer Who Suits Every Occasion," as I wear a snazzy suit that helps me to stand out from the crowd.

To transport your props, a wheeled suitcase can be very useful, and oversized tote bags (like IKEA bags) can hclp hold extra props and be used to carry your sound system.

When you set up, it can help to lay your props in the correct order on the stage in front of you. Lay out your props from right to left so from the audience's perspective your show is laid out correctly. Please also make sure the front row of your audience is not near enough to be able to grab your props.

Some jugglers buy all of their props in exactly the same color, while other jugglers like to buy a multitude of colors for everything. The choice is entirely yours—there is no right or wrong, although you may want to make sure your props don't clash with your chosen outfit or the background you are juggling against.

MUSIC & SOUND EQUIPMENT

If you are worried about what to say during your show, consider performing to a piece of music. You can find plenty of royalty-free music online. Pick a tune that you are not going to get tired of listening to, as you are going to be practicing a lot! The tempo of the music will set the speed of your routine, so a scarf routine might be best suited to a slow ballad, whereas club juggling could be done with a high-tempo dance track.

If you are speaking during your show, you will need a radio/wireless microphone in order to keep your hands free for juggling. Equipment that runs on rechargeable batteries is great because you can charge it fully before you leave the house rather than having to find a nearby outlet or use extension cords.

PRACTICE POINT: Don't give up! If you are on stage and drop during a certain routine, it may be worth attempting the trick a couple more times, with the audience getting more and more involved each time and willing you to nail the trick. You will end up with a bigger applause! Of course, if after the third or fourth attempt you sense the audience is beginning to lose interest, captivate them with a different trick and move on swiftly.

WHAT TRICKS TO PERFORM

Make a list of every trick you can do. If you have worked your whole way through this book, then you've got a good start!

Your primary focus is to be entertaining! If you only know a few tricks, then keep your routine short. You could, however, juggle the same trick higher and wider, faster and slower, as well as using large arm movements or hardly moving at all. The same trick can look a lot different if you add in body movements, change the tempo and make bigger throws. If you do have to return to the basic cascade pattern between every trick, make sure you move on swiftly to the next trick.

More isn't always better. If you become a nine-ball juggler, unless you can do lots of nine-ball tricks, the audience will be really impressed for the first five to ten seconds and then be wondering what your next trick is going to be. To put on an entertaining show, spend your time learning as many different tricks with as many different props as possible, rather than focusing on numbers of objects in the air. If you can perform with multiple props, start your show with the easiest prop and build up to the most difficult. There is, however, a funny way to perform nine-ball juggling (see the Routines section page 92).

NOTE:

- If you are able to greet people and chat with them before the show, they will be more likely to pay attention during your act and applaud extra loud!

APPLAUSE POINTS

Give the audience a chance to applaud your tricks. If you can add natural pauses to your routines, it gives the audience a chance to release some energy rather than saving it all up for one round of applause at the end. It also gives you a chance to take a deep breath and then continue. The best way to learn some pauses and poses is to watch video clips of the famous jugglers from Chapter 1.

NOTE:

- *Announce when you are about to perform your last routine so the audience knows when the show is coming to an end.*

WHAT TO DO IF YOU DROP

The audience should feel at ease throughout your show. If you look nervous, they will be nervous too. You have the power to make them feel at ease, and here are two ideas that will help you out.

- **Drop Version 1 - Nice:** Tell the audience you are new to juggling and that it is one of your very first performances, so you might accidentally drop at some point during the show. Kindly ask that they shout some words of encouragement at you whenever they see a mistake. You can then do some practice runs where you almost drop the ball but manage to recover, before actually doing a drop and listening to their encouragement.

- **Drop Version 2 - Nasty:** Let the audience know you may make a mistake at some point during the show, and if they spot a drop they should point at you and laugh as loudly as they can. Practice this a couple of times, letting them really go to town. Because you have asked them to be nasty, they are obeying you, so you are in full control.

Funny Drop Lines

If you drop during your routine, smooth things over with a joke!

- "It's not my fault. There was a sudden gust of wind. I think it was that lady/bloke in the third row!"

- Bend down to pick up the prop and say, "This act is beginning to pick up."

- Yell, "Look at that!" and point to the back of the room. As the audience turns around, quickly pick up the prop and continue juggling.

- "Wow, that's the first time that's ever happened … again."

- "If I didn't drop this much, the show would be a lot shorter. I'm giving you a great value for your money!"

HOW TO HANDLE A TOUGH AUDIENCE

If the audience isn't laughing or clapping very much, here are a couple of ideas to get them going.

- **Bounce Ball "Ha":** If the audience isn't laughing at your jokes and you need them to lighten up a bit, all you need is a bouncy juggling ball. Ask them to shout the word "Ha" every time the ball hits the ground. Throw the ball in the air and let it bounce. The "Ha" will get faster and faster, then the audience will realize they have been duped into making a laughing sound, which will make them laugh naturally. You can then tell them that you expect that response to all of your jokes!

- **Bounce Ball "Clap":** The technique is the same as above, except request that the audience clap their hands once for each time the ball is bounced. The audience will eventually realize that they are applauding, and you can remind them that you would like to hear more of that after all of your tricks!

ROUTINES

Putting together a routine of tricks and jokes can be intimidating. Here are some ready-to-go routines you can use in your show.

Nine Ball Juggling

You will need three tennis ball canisters. Put a bit of tape over the lids so they don't fly off when you juggle them! Tennis ball canisters will behave like juggling clubs, so you can flip them end over end. You can also use the following joke:

"Ladies and Gentlemen, would you like to see some nine-ball juggling?"

Audience replies: "Yes!"

"Well, is there anyone here who can juggle nine balls?"

Audience replies: "No."

"Oh well, never mind … "

Shrug your shoulders and move on to the next trick. Return a short while later with the three tennis canisters and begin juggling them. Some of the audience will realize you are now technically juggling nine balls, so you will get one wave of laughter, and then tell the rest of the audience that you are juggling nine balls and get an even bigger second wave of laughter!

Cleaning Up the Spotlight

If there is a spotlight on the stage, you can arrange this little routine with the person operating the lights.

Enter the stage with a brush, balance it on your chin (see page 81), then you can sweep the spotlight across the stage, and then "pack it up" (have the operator make it smaller and smaller) and put it in your pocket, at which point the room will go dark. You could then bring out some glow props!

Count the Bounces

Ask the audience to help you count the bounces of a bouncy juggling ball. After they have done it once, ask them to do it again. The number is likely to be different every time, so you can keep telling them they are wrong!

Disappearing Leg

Hold a large bath towel by the two top corners. Show that there is no hidden trapdoor on either side, and then hold the cloth in front of both feet. When you raise the towel, pick up one foot to make it appear that it has vanished. Then do the same with the opposite foot, and then finally exclaim that you can make both legs appear again—throw the towel up in the air and take a bow! You could even have your stage name sewn onto the towel— every bit of publicity helps!

Eat the Apple (Cheating)

You will need two balls and one apple. Chase a ball around trying to eat it for ten seconds, put the ball down, pick up a pad and paper and look thoughtful while you draw up a plan. Pick up both balls and the apple, but this time just juggle the two balls in one hand while you eat the apple using the other. This routine is even better with a banana! You could finish by throwing the banana over your shoulder and taking a bow, then as you leave the stage, slip on it.

Silly Person Stick

Point a stick at different people in the audience and say, "This stick will show me which people are really silly and which aren't." Say, "You are silly" repeatedly, and then make a show of realizing that you have the stick pointing the wrong way! A follow-up joke would be to point at someone and say, "This is a stick up!" Then point at someone else and say "This is a stick down," while pointing the stick at the ground!

WHAT'S NEXT?

I hope you have enjoyed learning how to juggle with a variety of objects. Your next steps are either to continue learning with them or to consider other props.

- Other types of props to manipulate: cigar box, devil stick, diabolo, spinning plate, spinning poi, rola-bola and unicycle.

- You could purchase a set of glow juggling equipment and perform all the tricks again but this time in the dark!

- Maybe add some magic to your routine. A vanishing purse will enable you to put three scarves in the purse and produce three balls (or make them disappear entirely!).

- The best way to continue learning is by finding your nearest juggling clubs and conventions where you can meet many wonderful jugglers who will be honored to teach you the next steps. Visit the Clubs and Events pages of the following website to find what is happening near you: *www.jugglingedge.com*.

Thank you for letting me teach you these tricks. Keep it up!

ABOUT THE AUTHOR

My real name is Steve Thomson, but as this doesn't sound like an entertainer's name, I am also known as Stevie Vegas! I was born in 1977 and raised in Stirling, Scotland, and have lived in Northamptonshire, England, since 2008. I am known as "The Entertainer Who Suits Every Occasion" because I currently have 19 different snazzy suits that I wear when I perform!

On Christmas Day in 1993, I received in my Christmas stocking (along with an orange and some chocolate coins) a set of juggling balls. Within a few days I had mastered the basic cascade and was keen to find out more. I then discovered that there was a juggling club—Stirling Juggling Project—that met on a weekly basis just ten minutes from my house! My new friends were amazing and encouraging (as are most jugglers you are ever likely to meet), and taught me a variety of skills.

Up until I became a juggler, I didn't enjoy school or learning and was painfully shy, but this immediately changed when I became a juggler. I had found my passion! I realized that juggling was something I quite literally needed to "keep up," and I believe it can make a big difference in your life too!

I became a professional juggler in 2001, and have since performed over 2,000 times, as well as appearing on TV and at many festivals all over the United Kingdom. My main passion, however, is "Gospel Juggling," through which I use my God-given talents to spread the Word! I helped create and run Scotland's first-ever juggling charity, "Jump, Juggle, Jest" (1994–2006), and I later went on to run Stirling Juggling Project (2003–2006). I now attend Milton Keynes Jugglers Anonymous. I am also the author of "Yo-Yo" (published by Mini Maestro).

You can visit me at *www.jugglingworld.biz* and on Twitter (*@SteveJuggler*), where I share a joke a day. I have reached the finals of the 2019 UK Pun Championships! You can also find me on Instagram and Facebook (*@StevieVegasJuggler*), or search for Stevie Vegas.